Your Dream Home

ISBN: 978-1-7361469-2-7

Published by Sacred Bones Books, 2024

1 2 3 4 5 6 7 8 9 10

All requests and correspondence can be addressed to

Sacred Bones Books
144 N. 7th Street #413
Brooklyn, NY 11249

Home is the place where all your nightmares happen.

This book is a collection of screenshots from Zillow that I took between 2020 and 2024.

2 of 36

1 of 40

1 of 15

33 of 35
Valley - Catskill Region MLS

44 of 48

1 of 37

1 of 22

1 of 40

36 of 42

34 of 49
©TriadMLS

11 of 13

7 of 32
STOP

26 of 30
LOUIS VUITTON
GUCCI
PRADA
COACH
MICHAEL KORS
PRADA
GUCCI
LOUIS VUITTON
MCM
OneKey MLS

7 of 36
©2022 Global MLS

23 of 29

28 of 47

3 of 31

12 of 16
SUBLIME
4:20 by Sublime
Exclusively at Spencer's

BAR

18 of 19

12 of 21
GLOBAL MLS, Inc.

21 of 31
OneKey MLS

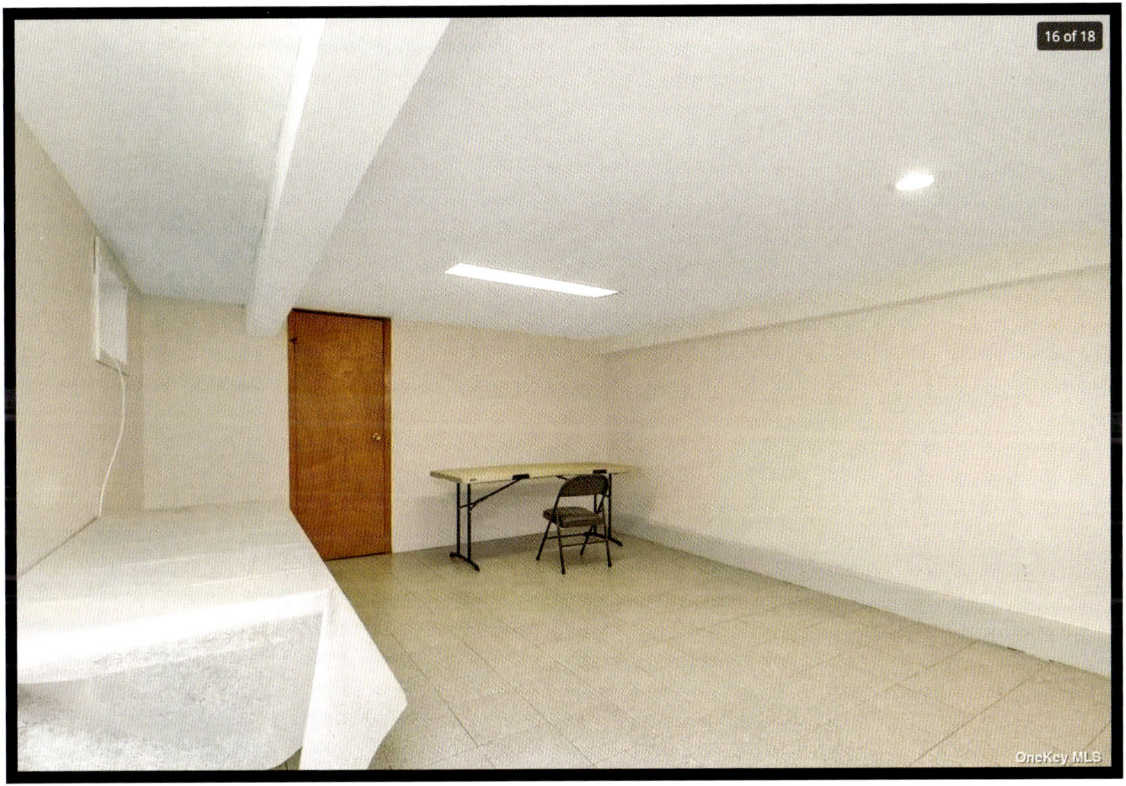
16 of 18
OneKey MLS

9 of 11

42 of 76
CGND

6 of 33
Hudson Valley -Catskill Region MLS

9 of 21

18 of 39
CGND

3 of 7
OneKey MLS

13 of 14
MLSLI

21 of 25

41 of 79
©2022 Global MLS

31 of 79
MOONSHINE JUNKIES
©2022 Global MLS

39 of 45
CGND
Columbia Greene
Northern Dutchess

8 of 15

©2023 Global MLS

22 of 34
Region MLS

12 of 28

18 of 22

21 of 36
OneKey MLS

10 of 31

27 of 40

15 of 45
CGND
Columbia Greene Northern Dutchess

18 of 28

23 of 71
SJ6RMLS

7 of 30
You + Me

9 of 9
1 lexi 2
GOD
07/04/2023 09:54:15 AM

8 of 23
GOOD
MORNING
FAM

12 of 20
FULL SEND

20 of 29
Family

27 of 56
SLAVE QUARTERS

26 of 27
NOOB
SLAYER
OneKey MLS

12 of 18
GO BROWNS

46 of 69
Staten Island Multiple Listing Service, Inc.

49 of 71
SEX AND THE CITY

13 of 23
WESLO
MLSLI

29 of 36
DEDICATION
ENJOY THE RIDE
MIND
MATTER

56 of 69
Staten Island Multiple Listing Service, Inc.

23 of 35
Hudson Valley -Catskill Region MLS-

52 of 87
bright MLS
BERKSHIRE HATHAWAY
BH
HS
HOMESERVICES

19 of 20
OneKey MLS

25 of 27
Smith
WEIL-McLAIN

32 of 55
©2022 Global MLS

6 of 33
OneKey MLS

36 of 50

11 of 28
Staten Island Multiple Listing Service, Inc.

6 of 10
©2023 Property of LCAR

25 of 32
OneKey MLS

18 of 27
OneKey MLS

25 of 38

32 of 32
OneKey MLS

16 of 29
Hudson Valley -Catskill Region MLS

27 of 66

4 of 23

17 of 36
©2022 Global MLS

7 of 18

16 of 18

3 of 12

22 of 29
OneKey MLS

2 of 12

5 of 12

16 of 35
CGND

13 of 22

24 of 26

1 of 5
New Construction
SJSRMLS

John Wilson is a Queens, NY based documentarian most well known for his HBO show *How To with John Wilson.*